WHEN IS A GOAT JUST A GOAT?

ROBBIE BYERLY

2   When there is just one animal, it goes by just one name.

But with two or more of the same animal,
that name is not the same.

4 Many animals live in groups.

It is what they like to do.

So when they are in a group...

...their names are something new.

All of these frogs are an army.

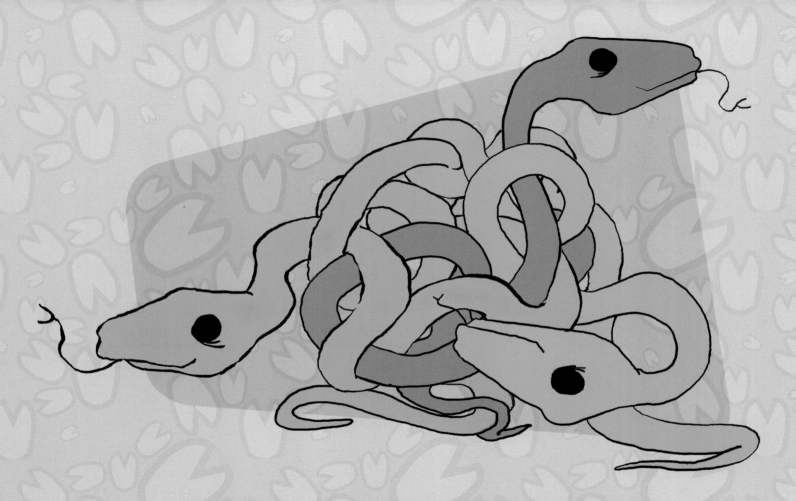

And all of these snakes are a knot.

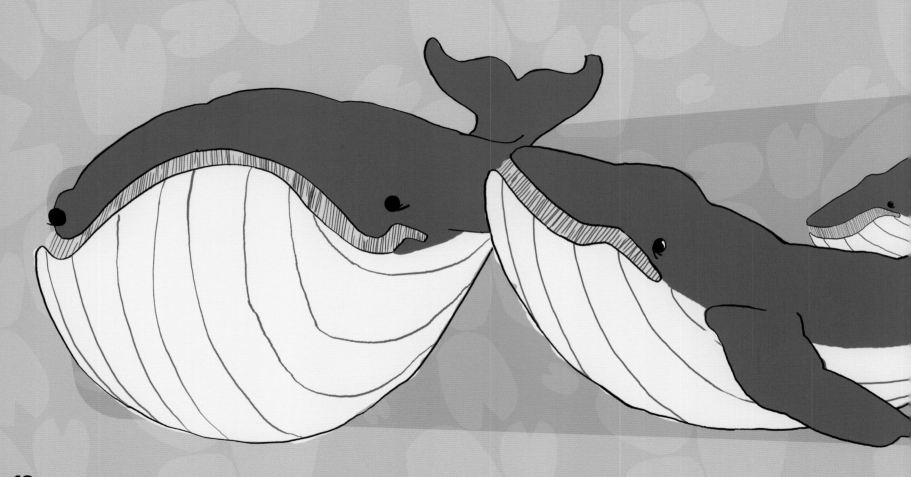

All of these whales are a mob.

All of these birds are a flock.

A group of camels can be a flock, and so can a group of sheep. Look at that flock of bats. A flock can't be beat.

13

14 These cows are in a herd, and so are these geese.

Same as the elephants. Same as the buffalo and, again, same as the sheep!

Now the hippos are a crash.

The lions are a pride.

But what about the goats?

Are they a flock, a herd, or a tribe?

They have all of these names...

...when they are not on their own.

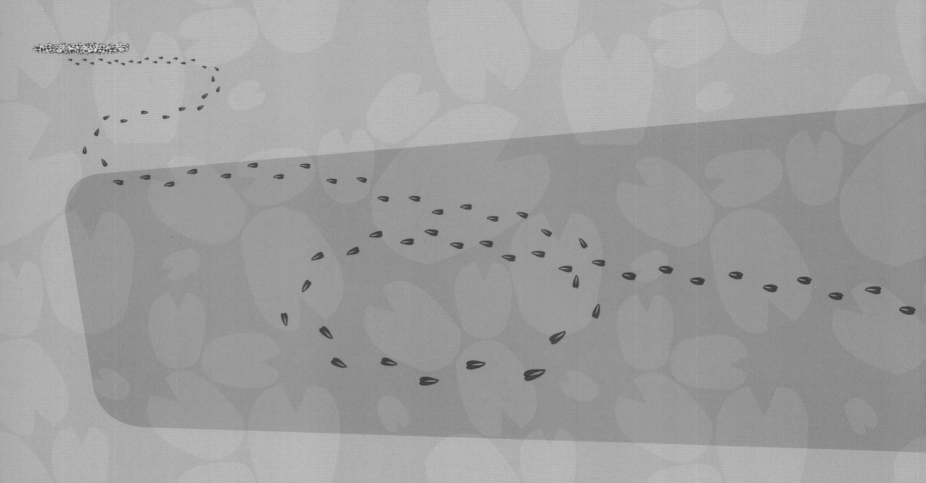

But a goat is just a goat...

...when it is all alone.

USE THE WORDS YOU KNOW
TO READ NEW WORDS!

eat	came	at	lots
meat	same	cat	lot
seat	lame	cash	not
beat	**name**	**crash**	**knot**

TRICKY WORDS

their   something   again   own   more   just